Pat's Map

by Lucy Shepard
illustrated by Olivia Cole

Core Decodable 14

McGraw Hill Education

Bothell, WA • Chicago, IL • Columbus, OH • New York, NY

MHEonline.com

Send all inquiries to:
McGraw-Hill Education
8787 Orion Place
Columbus, OH 43240

ISBN: 978-0-02-134566-3
MHID: 0-02-134566-X

Printed in the United States of America.

2 3 4 5 6 7 8 9 DOC 20 19 18 17 16 15

Pat's map sits on a mat.

Pat taps the map.

Sam stamps on Pat's map.

Sam taps Pat's map.

Sam hits Pat's map.

Sam nips Pat's map!